footy

AN AUSSIE RULES DICTIONARY

First published 1983 by Sun Books
THE MACMILLAN COMPANY OF AUSTRALIA PTY LTD
107 Moray Street, South Melbourne 3205
6 Clarke Street, Crows Nest 2065

Associated companies and representatives
throughout the world

Reprinted 1983, 1985 (twice), 1986, 1989 (twice), 1990

National Library of Australia
cataloguing in publication data

Dunstan, Keith.
Footy, an Aussie Rules dictionary.
ISBN 0 7251 0404 X.
1. Australian football—Dictionaries. I. Hook, Jeff, 1928– . II. Title.
796.33′6′03

Printed in Hong Kong

To all those who have heard the call of footy

footy

AN AUSSIE RULES DICTIONARY
BY KEITH DUNSTAN
ILLUSTRATED BY JEFF HOOK

Academy award

A

Academy Award If a player turns on a brilliant acting performance so gifted in artistry that he convinces an umpire that he deserves a free kick, then he has done an 'Academy Award job'.

Administrator A new creature at football clubs. He doesn't know anything about football, but he knows a helluva lot about money.

Admission Charge The one price that is perfectly indexed. It goes up every year.

Adrenalin Solution produced by adrenal glands when body receives a fright or is under stress. Commentators appear to pump buckets of the stuff, particularly during the time-on period.

Aerial Ping Pong The name lovingly bestowed on the national game by its admirers in Sydney.

Amateurs Back in the dreamtime of the last century all footballers were amateurs. The theory was that you played football because you loved the game. When payment became rife in the 1890s the purists argued that once you started paying a footballer, gamblers would pay him more to lose. There are still amateurs here and there, but like virgins in Kings Cross, they are hard to find.

Anti-Football League A large and growing band of honest, devoted, sincere people who believe that football makes life unbearable during winter. The AFL has a bigger membership

Aerial ping pong

Anti-Football League
DOWN
WITH
FOOTBALL

than any VFL club. Members have a badge that resembles a small red cube. It is symbolic of a football that will not bounce. When worn on a lapel or blouse, other members quickly identify it and recognize that here is a chance for an intelligent conversation.

Apologize

It did happen once. The remarkable event took place on the Melbourne Cricket Ground. There was a nice young amateur chap with the Demons. He had just arrived from Melbourne Grammar School. He pushed a Collingwood ruckman in the back and apologized. The shock reverberated around the ground.

Association

The true great football mother before the VFL was formed in 1896. Now you play for the VFA if you are not good enough for the League. The Association plays on Sundays, and like the emu and the ostrich has no use for wings.

Australian Rules Football

A game invented by the Melbourne Cricket Club to give its players some exercise during the winter months. Now no serious cricketer would play it for fear of being maimed.

Autumn

A beautiful time of the year when the air is full of optimism. Six recruits have come down from the country, eight have been bought for five million dollars from interstate. They are all young Buntons, Dyers, Colemans and Hudsons. They can kick a hundred metres with either foot and are certain to take the Brownlow first up. The coach has announced that this is our year, and it is at least six weeks before you hit the bottom of the ladder.

Autumn

B

Back	Backs are the noble, redoubtable defenders, but there are other meanings. As John O'Grady once said, 'Back is that part of a man's body that every other bastard ought to keep off.'
Bad Trot	A bad trot is a crook run. When you're having a bad trot or a crook run you haven't won a match since Cazaly was a kid.
Ball-hungry	Nothing to do with a passion for eating meatballs. It is important for all players to be eager, to be ravenously ball-hungry. More upper-crust sports announcers, such as you find on the ABC, prefer to describe it as 'having a desire for the ball'.
Ball-up	A method for resolving the umpire's helpless confusion.
Banana	A ball kicked off the wrong foot in the heat of battle. Like a heat-seeking sidewinder missile, uncannily it goes straight to the target. If the goal is yours, the banana kick is an example of superb, scientific skill handled with subtle accuracy. From the opposition, of course, it's a bloody fluke.
Bankruptcy	You buy fifteen footballers so that your team can make the final five. Their earnings alone are more than your entire 1982 revenue. The brink of bankruptcy is something a club manager learns to live with. Lord, send us a new sponsor tomorrow! Anybody—it doesn't matter if he runs a string of massage parlours!

Banana

Barracking	A method for exorcizing your pent-up emotions and neurotic beliefs on thirty-six innocent creatures who happen to be kicking a bladder around the field. Professor Ian Turner at the Ron Barassi Memorial Lecture gave the prime example of barracking. A St Kilda supporter, a can of beer in hand, called out to the umpire: 'You rotten, bloody, commo, poofter, mongrel bastard!' It's nice to get rid of all one's prejudices in one neat, clean sentence.
Bash Artist	You get all types of artists in Australian folklore and the most famous is the bullshit artist, but every team needs its hatchetman, its executioner, its bash artist.
Bawll	In non-football English, 'ball'. The cry of 'bawll' is an articulate scream from the crowd. It means that a gentleman from the opposing team has been in possession of the ball for an unconscionable period, even as long as two seconds.
Behind	A behind is worth one point, a goal six. Just when you need goals in a hurry you'll find that your full forward, the one that costs you 500 dollars a game, has lost sight of his goal and is trying to win the match on points.
Blind Freddy	The ultimate no-hoper who always possesses more wisdom than the coach, the selection committee and the team captain. 'We wooder won the match if only they'd swung the Gorilla to centre arf forward. Even Blind Freddy could see that.'
Blue	A stoush, an unfriendly argument. Always available in large numbers at football matches. The best way to get

Barracking

Behind

into a blue is to stand behind the opposition's goal and express a wholesome unbiased opinion.

Boos Heard to their best advantage on Grand Final day. The rising crescendo of 120,000 humans booing the umpire at the Melbourne Cricket Ground is unquestionably the most awesome tribal sound to be heard in the Southern Hemisphere.

Boot One never kicks a football, one boots it, or sends it, or delivers it, or swings into the attack, and on richly eloquent occasions one even sinks the slipper.

Boots One time a football boot was a majestic thing that weighed several kilos. It was like a military boot, with caps like armour plating over the toes and ankles. Maybe the massive proportions of the old boot is why the players of another generation seemed to kick further and straighter. Now the footy boot is cut down at the sides. It is light and delicate; like the sneakers of a burglar, it is made for speed. Naturally, it must have stripes down the side to advertise some manufacturer, rich and foreign.

Booze Efforts have been made to restrict it, right back to the days of lace-up guernseys, but football and beer go together like toes and toenails. It is booze that has given footy crowds their eloquence. Maybe booze is necessary to give a human being a reason for standing outside in wind, cold and rain on a winter afternoon watching thirty-six other humans do violence to each other. It has been said that the most evocative Australian sound is that of an empty can gently clanking its way down the concrete steps of the MCG.

Bounce	To be there for the bounce is a term that goes deep into Australian folklore. It means the start of any enterprise, from the tapping of an 18-gallon keg through to the opening session of the High Court. One has to be there for the bounce. It is also the start of an Australian Rules football match.
Boundary Umpire	A poor creature who needs the speed of an Olympic sprinter, the endurance of a marathon runner, and as he does that pretty dash to the centre after the kicking of a goal, the style of a Nureyev. It is necessary for aspiring field umpires to serve their apprenticeship on the boundary, because there they learn the finer points of the game from the crowd.
Brownlow Medal	An annual TV vote orgy done in defiance of all the newspaper and multi-media votes. The secret-ballot votes of the umpires are called out, round by round—although, cunningly, it seems to happen with the maximum climax towards the finish. Umpires hardly ever notice far-off people like full backs and full forwards. The award is for 'best and fairest', but the number of great players who have not won a Brownlow could fill three trainloads of the *Spirit of Progress*. Brownlowless Jack Dyer once said the medal goes to the greatest milksop.

C

Carlton	Carlton used to boast Sir Robert Menzies as its number one ticket holder. It looks upon itself as a slightly upper-class club. It has the dreariest of nicknames—'the Blues'—which only goes to prove that nicknames are unimportant when it comes to inspiring passion, because Carlton has won the VFL flag fifteen times. Very nearly the greatest news story of the 1960s was the stealing of the Melbourne captain, Ron Barassi, to become the Carlton coach.
Carn	A pathetic plea frequently used in times of great perturbation of spirit—e.g. Carn Esserdon, Carna Tigers, Carnya bloody lotta no-hopers.
Centre Square	An exclusive club area for four players of each team while the umpire is bouncing the ball. After the bounce it becomes as busy as a stop-work meeting at Festival Hall.
Charging	A method for defeating your opponents without the tiresome encumbrance of a football.
Charisma	Every footballer needs it. Particularly when he goes on to do detergent, deodorant and underpants commercials.
Cheer Squad	A group that hangs banners over fences, puts streamers over players' races and dresses in abominable clothes. In its more refined form the cheer

squad consists of near-naked maidens who dance up and down with pompoms. They are more agreeable to watch than the football.

Cherry, Two bites of the
Microphone speak for 'He fumbled the bloody thing.'

Circuit Training
According to the definition, 'A programme which aims at the progressive development of muscular and cardio-vascular fitness'. In other words, exhausting the poor bastards without even using a football.

Clearance
That mystical thing which never happens when the player wants it. If he's no good it comes too soon. If he's extra good they won't let him go so that he can make some money before his knees crack. If he's ultra good and the club is broke, they will trade him for the cash. Ultimately the poor lad is sold like a heifer at the stockyards. His best hope is to get into TV like Lou Richards.

Coach

A murderous profession. Like Roman Emperors, coaches suffer from a lack of longevity. The average length of tenure in office is less than three seasons. In the Victorian Football League there are twelve senior coaches, so at the end of each season there remains one brilliant coach and eleven others who are incompetent, ineffective men who failed to listen to the good advice of the president, secretary and selection committee. Coaches have to be diplomatic, they have to be brilliant orators with silver tongues on a par with Gielgud, Olivier and Richard Burton. They need the tactical skills of a Rommel, the drive of a General Patton, the ruthlessness of Genghis Khan and the persuasive skills of an Avon lady. They must be capable of turning timid, quarter-skilled half-witted 19-year-olds into brilliant, fearless heroes. Even though paunchy and aged they need to look good in shorts, they need style and panache on television, and in committee rooms they need more political skill than Henry Bolte. They are recompensed for their services at less than half the rate of a competent ruck rover.

Collingwood

Industrial suburb famous for the manufacture of shoes, SP bookies, two-up and a football team called the Magpies—a team blessed with more tradition than the Grenadier Guards, Royal Horse Artillery and United States Marines combined. Time was when children born in the Collingwood district were expected to sign form fours swearing eternal loyalty before leaving maternity hospital. The winning of a Collingwood guernsey was always considered on a par with winning the Order of Merit or the Nobel Prize. If a Justice of the

High Court had also played football for Collingwood, upon receiving his eternal reward, naturally, the newspapers in their obituaries would mention first that he was a Collingwood footballer. However, only the old and venerable can remember when Collingwood last won a premiership. The year was 1958. The team, like Flinders Street Railway Station, has aged beautifully.

Colliwobbles A deep-seated, infectious virus that has affected Collingwood since the late 1950s. Almost everything has been tried, from using Gough Whitlam as number one ticket holder through to (shudder) the appointment of a coach who has never played for the Magpies and (double shudder) the invasion of a pep-up team from south of the Yarra.

Contract A terrific deal. The social club has been urging you to buy a top player all the year. So you buy a ruckman from interstate. He costs you half a million dollars over five years. He's on the front and back pages of the newspapers for five days. For six weeks he doesn't get a kick. The seventh week you drop him to the thirds.

Conveniences At football grounds, usually, anything but. It is worse for females. Often it can take as long as a whole quarter of waiting just to get convenient.

Coterie The football mafia. The mysterious group that lurks in the background, provides all the loot, and entices down the new recruit from Scungywallop who can kick a steer a hundred metres with either foot. The coterie also tries to sack the coach before he has had time to read the paper in the morning.

Conveniences

Cricket

Coulter Law	A naïve idea that all footballers are equal. In the early days they even thought that they should all be paid three pounds a week. It was a damned nuisance really, because it also meant that you had to provide your star ruckman with a house and a car, and fly his girlfriend down from Sydney every week.
Cricket	An inconvenience that not only owns sporting grounds but occupies them, thus making it difficult to extend the football season to the full twelve months.

D

Day, On the	Essential equipment for any coach when speaking to the press after the match. Never says 'The bastards killed us.' The correct form is this: 'They won because they were better on the day.'
Desire	Desire for the ball, absolutely essential on Saturday afternoons. Desire for females on Friday nights? Absolutely out of the question.
Done Like a Dinner	A message designed to give the impression that your team had conspicuous lack of success.
Drop Kick	Back in the dreamtime this was the most beautiful kick in football. It had accuracy, it had style, and it had range. Now, like standing up for ladies in trams, it has gone out of fashion, and the young players don't know how to do it anyway.
Dropping the Ball	Being caught to stay home and do the gardening.

Desire

E

Elbow

A superb, very hard instrument that God obviously designed for flattening other footballers. It has this beautiful advantage. In the pack an umpire cannot see an elbow as easily as a flailing fist.

End of Season Trip

This is the reward, the carrot that is dangled before the team all season. You would expect that maybe twenty players would merit this honour. But come the end of the season the team has grown to the size of the Argentine Army, with coaches, managers, runners, rubber-downers, coterie money-grubbers, club doctor, club accountant, president, secretary, committee . . . The more successful the team the further the trip—Hawaii, Los Angeles, the Caribbean. All through the season publicity is relished and adored. End of season trips get the cover-up like Watergate. Eventually players return to their wives, even worse relics than they were after the Grand Final.

End of season trip

Eucalyptus

Esky Instrument used for carrying sustenance into the ground. In older civilizations citizens rent their clothes and tore their hair. Australians in moments of extreme grief break up their Eskies.

Essendon Foundation member of the VFL. They used to be called the 'Same Olds' or the 'Blood-stained Niggers', then the 'Bombers'. Now more often they answer to the 'Dons', but naturally the correct way to pronounce the name is 'Esserdon'. Curiously, they played at Jolimont until 1920. Now their headquarters are at 'Windy Hill' in Essendon, where on a typical July afternoon one can experience whistling draughts of fresh air unequalled outside Antarctica.

Eucalyptus The oil from gum leaves is used to anoint the limbs of footballers. Trainers rub them down before and during matches. It loosens the joints and gives freedom to the muscles, but also it has magical, mystic qualities and is the essential ingredient Australians must have before going into battle. New Zealanders chant the haka, Ockers rub themselves with eucalyptus. Furthermore, it sends the adrenalin racing in any true Australian female. There is an aphrodisiac quality about any warm, eucalyptus-smelling Australian footballer. Get him before his knees begin to go.

F

Fathers Haunted creatures who live out their fantasies through their sons. They are out there on the ground in the cold and the damp, on Tuesday evening, on Wednesday evening or Thursdays. They had the agony of watching whether junior would make the final training list, now there's the rush to the radio or the television on Thursday nights just to make sure he has been selected again for Saturday. Fathers attend the club meetings, they are always present for the Sunday morning socials and barbecues, drinking the beer devotedly to keep up club funds. It is a relentless, time-consuming occupation. It is worse for their wives. They can't stand the sight of the wreck that comes home every Saturday night—not the father, that's bad enough, but the wounded, bruised son who limps through the door.

Final Five

The ultimate end of the agony. One miserable decimal point can mean that your team hasn't made it. This usually happens after you have already bought your tickets for the finals.

Final Siren

Sense of relief like the lifting of a death sentence if your team happens to be in front. Sense of relief even greater if it means that your husband is going to turn off the television set and return to the world.

Fitness Test

Your full forward is suffering from concussion, a trifling skull fracture, a severed Achilles tendon, a bruised groin and a broken arm, but he gets a fitness test on Friday afternoon just to make sure he can play on Saturday afternoon.

Fitzroy

The club has won the flag eight times, but hardly anyone around is old enough to remember the last illustrious occasion in 1944. Fitzroy holds some sort of record for moving around. Originally it played right there in its working-class heart at Brunswick Street, Fitzroy. In 1967 it tried sharing Princes Park with more upper-class Carlton. Then in 1970 it shifted to St Kilda's Junction Oval. Once upon a time Fitzroy had the awesome name 'The Gorillas'. Then they changed it to 'The Lions', which makes them sound more like a Rotary Club, and they haven't won a flag since.

Fitness test

Floggers

Flat Out like a Lizard Drinking	Useful alternative phrase for shirt-front job. It means that your star has just been stretched out horizontal, face down on the turf.
Floggers	Bundles of shredded paper attached to a stick. During moments of emotional intensity, such as the scoring of a goal or the execution of a tiresome enemy ruckman, one thrashes them up and down in a vertical plane. It helps.
Footscray	Bulldogs, quixotic, unpredictable, dynamic in May, awful in August. Yet they have been known to bite. Bulldog fans look back with tears of nostalgia to 1954, their one and only flag. Even more tearfully they look back to 1961. That year never-won Hawthorn beat them in the Grand Final. Bulldogs change their administration and their coaches as often as most people change their clothes.
Footsteps	Ultimately it hits them all. In World War I it was shell shock. In World War II, you went troppo. The poor coot is no longer game to go for a mark. He's hearing footsteps—the Ben Hur charge of the hulk behind who is about to kill him.
Footy	Ball game played on muddy ovals to entertain thousands of people who know more about it than the players. It is essential to pronounce the word correctly: 'foody'—rhymes with 'goody'.
Forearm	A wonderful weapon attached to most human beings by an elbow. Skilfully directed at close range it can even crush bones. Far less obvious than a fist or a foot, and frequently it can be put to effective use without meriting the busybody attention of umpires.

Free Kick	An odd term. Usually you have to earn it by putting your back in front of somebody's hand, holding your crotch in agony or falling on your face in the mud.
Fuchsias	The old name for Melbourne. There was the terrible fear that someone might call them the Pansies, so during the 1930s they changed their name to the Demons.
Full Forward	The most famous Australian Rules story concerns a sign outside a church in Hawthorn, which said: 'What would you do if God came to Hawthorn today?' A graffiti artist scrawled underneath: 'Move Peter Hudson to centre half forward.' A full forward is a creature who is supposed to lead out with the acceleration of a Harrier jet leaving the deck of an aircraft carrier. His leaping skills must be such that he can claw the ball down from six metres aloft. He must have the shooting accuracy of an Exocet guided missile and his fans expect him to kick at least 100 goals a year. One time he could be slim and lean. Not any more. If he kicks any goals at all he is marked for death by terrorist ruckmen, so he must be built like Conan the Barbarian. His chances of getting a Brownlow Medal are nil. Umpires can never see that far up the field, except when they are making a report.

G

Geelong	Right from the time when it thought it could be Port Phillip's number one port, Geelong has never liked

Footsteps

Free kick

Melbourne. Nor has Melbourne ever enthused about Geelong. Mutual dislike is an excellent basis for a football match. The Geelong special train back and forth on Saturdays has always been loaded with emotionally charged citizens. Originally Geelong was called the 'Seagulls' or the 'Pivotonians'. Legend has it that once a black cat crossed the ground and immediately Geelong won the match. They have been the 'Cats' ever since.

General Manager

Once upon a time clubs were run by club secretaries. Business organizations call for a general manager. The next step will be for clubs to become public companies with shares listed at the stock exchange and prices rising and falling according to the dash and doom of fortunes on the League ladder.

Getting Your Act Together

Gathering together half a dozen cans, finding the most comfortable seat in the house, taking up a secure position in front of the TV set and not expecting any interruptions for several hours.

Giveaways

There are lots to be had in football. The footballers who consent to go on television programmes are lathered with gifts—bottles of champagne, shirts, tins of fruit cake, boxes of dog food, electric toasters . . . But best of all are the end-of-season gifts for those who win the multitude of votes and medals offered by TV stations, radio and newspapers. A smart conspicuous footballer can win as many as three automobiles and a motor boat in one bonny September.

Goal

Goal	Six points, the ultimate desire in Australian Rules football. In radio parlance it can be referred to in various ways. He's kicked a major. It's through. It's through the big sticks. Or, in moments of extreme exultation, it's gone through the high diddle diddle.
Goal Sneak	If he's yours he's the brilliant fellow who roams loose around the goal square and craftily steals goals. If he belongs to the opposition, what the hell is the bastard doing untailed and why didn't we squash him in the first quarter?
Goal Square	An area in which almost all thirty-six players can be seen at any one time.
Guernsey	The ultimate honour in Australia. When you get a guernsey you are in the team. At the beginning of the season there is a mystic rite, such as might have been carried out by the ancient Druids, when on the special club night the players receive their guernseys. The ceremony at which the Queen confers the Order of the Garter pales by comparison.
Gunner	Gunner win tomorrer. Gunner get in the final five. Gunner get a forward that can kick straight. Gunner get a bloody new selection committee. Gunner talk to me missus some time—that's if I get a chance after World o' Sport tomorrer.
Guts and Determination	Ninety-nine point nine per cent of all coach addresses include the demand for 'gutserntermination'. Except in more refined clubs where coaches make an appeal for 'intestinal fortitude'.

H

Hacking

When one's football boot 'accidentally' makes contact with the opposing player's shin instead of the football.

Handball

It's the old game of keepings-off. For sides that can't kick, it passes for team-work.

Hawthorn

Once upon a time the Hawks' followers seemed very nice people from a well-mannered suburb. The team played on a ground that was really too narrow and awkward for a good football match. Occasionally the Hawks won a home game because nobody else understood its mysteries, but normally they were crushed on any given Saturday. Then they started acquiring people like John Kennedy, Peter Hudson and 'Lethal' Leigh Matthews, and they became disagreeable to everyone. Hawthorn won its first premiership in 1961. Seismic reverberations from the area were noted 500 kilometres away.

Heart

Has nothing to do with love. Coaches are always describing players as having great heart. It means that they tirelessly, devotedly, self-destructively, give themselves to the cause, hammering away at the game for all quarters. At the office on Monday they usually sleep soundly until lunchtime.

Holding the Ball

Some players touch the ball so infrequently that when it comes into their arms it is like a mother holding her baby, it is impossible to part with something so precious. It is also known as hatching.

Home Advantage	Nobody else dares take your regular seat in the grand-stand.

Holding the ball

Interchange

I

Instant Replay	The new marvel of science—you don't have to watch the game any more. If anything serious, dramatic or marvellous happens, they will show it to you with the instant replay on the great electronic scoreboard.
Interchange	This is a recent innovation. Back in pre-war years the club had to pay only eighteen players. Now, apart from the reserves, there are two spare players. They are not there merely to replace the wounded. Interchangers are there to throw into action to replace players who are performing miserably. The interchange is handy for your once brilliant star. His battle-scarred body, like a rocket, is good only for spectacular bursts.
Interference	Used to be a carefully rounded euphemism for what you did to a lady who is not your wife. Now it is a euphemism for what you do to a player who no longer has the ball.
Interstate	Every season there are interstate matches, a tiresome interruption. State selectors pick one or two top players from each side to play for the state. Out in darkest Collingwood, or nicest North Melbourne, this causes fury. Football there is a completely introverted game. They believe interstate football only serves to disrupt the local home games. They don't want their players to be champions of Australia or champions of the world. How can they be? Melbourne is the world already.

K

Kelly, Ned, Game as	A remarkably brave footballer.
Kiggit	Or even **Kiggit Ya Stoopid Baarstid**. A piece of helpful advice to a player who feels he has remarkable athletic gifts and it is better to deliver the ball by hand.
Killed 'Em	By remarkable good luck we just managed to win by two points.
King Hit	A profoundly large hit delivered to the jaw, preferably not seen by the umpire.
Kissing	Goals are such rare and wonderful events in soccer that players display their affection for each other by exchanging kisses. Australian Rules players have been less certain of their virility. Richards, Dyer, Barassi, Polly Farmer and their entire generation indulged in very little kissing. But times are changing. Now we are getting some delicious hugs after the scoring of goals.
Knee	A somewhat inefficient hinge designed for humans when they operated on all fours. Clearly God never envisaged an activity as peculiar as Australian Rules Football, with his creatures flying high in the air, then being assaulted as they reach the earth. Knees on the average last maybe fifty games. If they were horses at Flemington the footballers would be taken out and shot. Instead they are handed over to highly paid surgeons who indulge in cartilage removal and such. Polly Farmer's knee was the biggest news story for the entire decade of the 1960s.

Kelly, Ned, Game as

Kissing

L

Ladder A slippery slide organized for the weekly glory and humiliation of football clubs. In Melbourne the same newspaper will publish the League ladder as often as eight times a week, frequently four times in the same issue.

Loyalty A strange, indefinable thing. A player's loyalty is in direct proportion to the size of his contract. Some players have so much loyalty they can spread it across five clubs before they hang up their boots.

Loyalty
$

Mark

M

Mannnn	Evocative crowd howl. Meaning that the opposition has been indulging in a little play without the luxury of the presence of the ball.
Mark	A method for gaining a free kick from the umpire. In order to be seen, your mark needs to be as spectacular as possible. In other more amiable sports the player merely catches the ball.
Mark of the Day	Worth two bottles of bubbly, a packet of detergent and six cans of free cat food from Lou Richards on Sunday morning television.
MCG	This is the cathedral, the centre of the archdiocese in Australia. It is the home for two permanent congregations—Richmond and Melbourne. It is quite common in religion to worship strange objects, pieces of wood, stone or even cows. Australians prefer a piece of leather, or often a horse. The most sacred rite in the archdiocese takes place late in September. The cathedral is filled and the collection is satisfactory.
Melbourne	The Demons, a football team owned by the Melbourne Cricket Club. The club even claims to have invented Australian Rules Football as a method for keeping their cricketers fit during the winter months. Indeed Melbourne in the old days always had a slightly upper-crust flavour. If public-school boys dared to drift from all-amateur football, most likely they would play for Melbourne.

Members	An area where there is a reasonable chance of finding clean lavatories.
Merri Creek Soil	Thick, black, gluey soil with strange, almost baffling qualities. It has been used for cricket pitches in Melbourne for more than a century. On most cricket grounds it has built up in the centre, anything up to a metre deep. Come the wet weather it turns into an impenetrable bog, so awful even a Leopard tank would fail to make its way through. Umpires would not dare bounce a ball on it. The ball would be swallowed into its murky depths. This is why players find Waverley so dull. There is no challenge of Merri Creek splodge in the centre.

Merri Creek soil

Monday After

The year is full of Mondays-after, but no other is quite like the Monday after Grand Final Day. There is a terrible hole in your life. The garden has not been looked at since last March. It looks like a tangled rain-forest 20 kilometres out of Lae. The gutters are full of leaves. The house has to be painted. You were going to change it from Collingwood colours to Hawthorn anyway. Your wife already is making sarcastic remarks. 'I'd like you to meet Sarah, she has grown four inches since you last saw her. And . . . oh . . . your mother died just before the Carlton–Hawthorn match but I thought it best not to advise you until after the Grand Final, first things first.' It's hell. Not a game worth looking at until February at least. But all is not lost: they'll start sacking coaches again next week.

Mother

It is not easy being the mother of a footballer. She is constantly washing socks, shorts and track-suits, and every footballer has fifteen guernseys. Constantly he is being injured, so she nurses the bruises, the sprains, washes away the blood. All the way through the fourths, thirds, seconds, she urges him to give it away. Is it all worth it? Ah, but now he is a star. There is kudos, prestige to be had at bridge, or in the supermarket. Your boy is famous, he is even advertising Crunchy Crunch biscuits on television. Then when you die you get your name in the *Herald*. And why not? You are the mother of a footballer.

Mug

Generic term for anybody in an opposing team. Frequently mugs are not unknown even on your own team. You also get bloody mugs, and in extreme cases bloody mug galahs.

N

National Football League — An organization of all Australian Rules football bodies that wishes it had more power than the Victorian Football League.

National Pastime — Football, of course. Pastime is derived from 'pass the time', in other words a method for getting rid of the hours. A purist might even suggest that the national pastime is the national waste of time.

Night Football — A convenient method for television stations to boost their 'Australian' live content during the week and to draw in a heap of well-paid advertising.

Nobody Home — Out to lunch. Visiting his girlfriend. Back o' Bourke. Every mug galah is missing when you're trying to get a lead.

North Melbourne — Once potent VFA team, didn't come into the VFL until 1925. They operate from Arden Street, where the only item of picturesque beauty has been a gasometer. Once they were called Hotham, once they were called the 'shinboners' perhaps because of their skill in attacking shins. Now they have the milder name 'The Roos'. Nearly always they were at the bottom of the ladder, until with a combination of money, Allen Aylett and Ron Barassi they won the 1975 VFL flag. It was an event of world significance on a par with the arrival of Halley's Comet. They have been hard to handle ever since.

National pastime

Outer

Number One

If you want to get on in politics, if you want to pick up quick prestige, become number one in a football club. For years it was traditional for the Victorian Governor to be number one at Richmond or Hawthorn. Gough Whitlam, who had no reason to have any interest in Victoria's recreational activities, became number one at two clubs, Geelong and Collingwood.

O

Old Footballer

A creature with misty eyes and arthritic knees. He tells stories well, and like King Harry at Agincourt, likes everyone to rue the day they were not present in 1932, '48, '58, or '68. That was a match indeed, when men knew how to play football.

Open Slather

A free-for-all, which the TV cameras never miss, a perfect item for the 7 o'clock news.

Opiate of the People

A term favoured by sociologists. Football is a religion that relieves boredom and keeps the masses off the streets right through the winter season.

Outer

The vast area where non-members sit or mostly stand. During World War II when the MCG was an Air Force camp the erks were in the Outer while the officers had the grander quarters in the Members. Time hasn't changed anything. This is the area still where you get the most life, the most colour, the most drunks, the best fights, the longest lavatory queues, where during the cricket season the drone of "Ave a go' comes plaintively all day, and during the winter 'Carna Tigers' or 'Call yourself a fuggin umpire?' If you are having trouble acquiring vituperative skills you learn quickly in the Outer.

Out of Bounds The area where you are certain to be lynched if you keep hollering for your beloved team.

P

Package Deal An arrangement to woo the new ruckman from interstate. He gets a house in Toorak, a job with BHP, a super luxury Commodore with air-conditioning, air transport home whenever he wants, and a girlfriend on Wednesday nights.

Passion Not easy to maintain throughout an almost interminable season. Yet passion can be built, just like physical fitness. Find out filthy things about the opposition. Listen to the most learned lavatory rumours. Quickly you will find out how they won all those classy players from Perth, Hobart and Adelaide. They got the money from the Mafia and the CIA. Work on the thoughts that their number one ruckman is the dirtiest behind-the-play hit-man in the League and that their centre half forward beats up his wife and kids every night before sleeping with a sleazy St Kilda barmaid. Concentrate on the thought that their full forward is gay and their full back is not only a Communist but against Princess Di and has even been heard to say disparaging things about the royal baby. The more passion you can generate, the more hate you can get out of your system.

Place Kick

A beautiful spectacle. The forward after winning his free kick places the ball on the ground, and like a bower bird carefully builds a nest with his egg pointed to the sky. All this can take up to ten minutes. Then he takes his running kick. It is supposed to achieve the accuracy of a guided missile. Alas, the place kick, like the drop kick, hardly ever happens now.

Pies An abbreviation for Magpies, a team that operates out of Collingwood, Victoria. The other sort of pie is the sacred diet, the item of food consumed at all football grounds. It is a curious item, indigenous to Australia. It has an outer shell that appears to be made of thin, damp cardboard. Inside there is a small lake of meat gravy, maybe three or four millimetres deep. Above the gravy and under the roof there is a vacant allotment. This is important. One takes a plastic bottle of tomato sauce and injects the nozzle like a hypodermic needle, thus filling the empty area with this caustic red fluid. Australians at an early age learn with brilliance how to eat these pies without spilling a drop of meat or sauce. The secret is to eat the pie while holding it partly in a paper bag. It is an Australian ceremony, conducted with all the grace and skill of a Spanish bullfight, and about equally as savoury.

Play On Somebody should have had a free kick, but you can't think who.

Preliminary Final Now that there is a final five, finals can be nigh interminable. The preliminary final is the final that comes before the Grand Final. Then if only a tie can be organized the football season can be pushed right into October.

President A wonderful position to have. He doesn't take the blame for the losses every Saturday. He just sacks everybody else.

Properties Division It is possible to live your entire life using only articles associated with your beloved football team. However, the cunning VFL has now patented all symbols. This

Queue
OUTER
CHANGE
TICKETS

means, whenever you dry yourself with a club towel, whenever you devotedly dry up the dishes with the club of your choice, wear a wig in the red, white and black stripes of St Kilda, whenever your baby loyally soils its club-oriented nappies, that the proceeds ultimately go to the League. Your car, house, even kitchen stove, can be done in club colours. However, changing clubs, particularly in mid-season, can be hideously expensive.

Q

Queue

A strange need for human beings to stand one behind the other. Common at football grounds, particularly during the finals period, when they have been known to do it, even in the most appalling weather, for a week on end. Rarely are queues necessary. However, psychologists say they give comfort. They fulfil a herd instinct, they provide a feeling of security, the reassurance of having made a right decision along with others in the queue.

Quid, Not the Full

A very sensitive term meaning that your ruckman, coach, president or whoever is not in full possession of his faculties.

R

Rainmaker	Microphone speak for ball projected vertically through the clouds like a space launch. It won't necessarily produce rain. That comes anyway.
Replay	It is impossible to see live matches on television the day they are played. However, Saturday nights are devoted to footy replays. The idea is to go to the football on Saturday afternoon, then hurry home quickly just to make sure everything you saw with your own eyes was perfectly accurate. You can even take in three whole matches on the footy replay. At Grand Final time the big match is played over and over again repeatedly on Saturday night, repeatedly on Sunday and all through the week. The serious admirer can get to see the Grand Final twenty times.
Report	A filthy lie perpetrated by umpires, boundary umpires and goalies about your beloved player. TV film serves only to double the lie. Cameras are renowned for getting the thing from the wrong angle.
Retire	One never retires, one hangs up one's boots.
Richmond	One of Australia's most historic clubs, dating back to the 1860s. At one time the players wore yellow, blue and black guernseys. They have long since adopted the more tasteful style of black with a yellow diagonal sash. Richmond was always a working-class suburb, if now somewhat gentrified, and the team has always had a reputation for unequalled ferocity. They are known as the 'eat 'em alive Tigers'. Such a reputation

Report

for cannibalism would be better in Sydney where Rugby players enjoy biting each other in the scrum. Richmond now shares the Melbourne Cricket Ground with the Demons. It has done nothing to make them more kindly.

Rover

Like a Christian who has much to do with lions, he needs to be remarkably brave, quick and cunning to survive. Rovers are supposed to run all the time and do most of the work. Ruckmen are there like telegraph poles; they knock the ball down to the rovers. It is useful if rovers are small—they don't have to bend so far to pick up the ball. They can also run between the muscle men's legs.

Rucks

They are supposed to be large and awesome and to inspire terror in the opposition. Also, like Mafia hit-men, they are there as a protection agency. Should any regrettable incident occur to a member of the home side it is the job of the ruckman to make sure that counter action takes place in the best and fairest manner that can be conducted out of line of sight of the umpire. Ruckmen, however, do have to run. That is, they have to be able to keep up with the play, so that when the umpire bounces the ball they are present to knock it down to the rovers.

Runner

A fleet-of-foot player, who never got in the team, either because he couldn't think or couldn't kick. He is used to send out messages to the captain, such as 'Unless you get some goals in the next five minutes you'd better find a new job like kamikaze pilot in the Israeli Air Force.'

Screamer
EEEEK

S

St Kilda

A football team strangely called 'The Saints'. Its home suburb was originally named after a sailing ship that visited Port Phillip when Melbourne was young. There is no record that a saint of that name ever existed. Nor is there much record of saintly behaviour in the St Kilda football team. Indeed, the team doesn't even play in the city it represents. It has moved down the scale to Moorabbin. Like the removal of the Dodgers baseball team from Brooklyn to Los Angeles, it was a move that was not easily forgiven.

Scoreboard

A large electrical object very useful for advertising tobacco, beer, footballs, Japanese motor cars, banks, insurance . . . and if you look carefully, also the score.

Screamer

An astro job, a cloud nudger, a back climber—indeed an extraordinarily high mark.

Shepherding

Putting out your arms to prevent the approach of the enemy. It saves you from the grubby business of having to go in and pick up the ball yourself.

Shirt-front

When you do a shirt-front job you iron out your opponent, you give him an altitude-zero treatment, you make him lower than a goanna's gut, you relocate him face-down in the mud. It is a scene particularly cherished by telecasters. A good shirt-front job is good for at least forty replays on prime news time.

Short of a Gallop

Your team never actually loses just through sheer inadequacy. There is another mystical reason, which implies 'if only things had been equal'. In other words they were short of a gallop.

Social Club

A drinking body usually devised in the hope that sufficient imbibing will make it possible to meet the new full forward's pay cheque.

South Melbourne

Once there was a great football team named South Melbourne. Back in celebrated years like 1933 and 1909 South Melbourne even won the premiership. South Melbourne and St Kilda were at either end of Albert Park Lake and they even fought their own private king-of-the-lake premiership. Now both teams have abandoned the lake and South Melbourne has flown to Sydney to become the Sydney Swans. Some see it as a missionary role, like a group of Baptists in Teheran trying to convert the followers of Islam. Others see it as a wonderful way of getting League footy onto Melbourne's Sunday TV. In Sydney it is OK to do wicked things like playing League footy on Sunday.

Spectator

What an extraordinary being! He chooses in mid-winter to go outside. He chooses to sit on a hard bench or stand in the rain for nigh on three hours. The comforts are sparse. If he wants a pie, a hot dog or a beer, or if he merely wants a lavatory, he has to elbow his way through humanity to stand in a queue. He has rowdy Ockers screaming in his ear. He could be playing a game of his own, like golf or tennis. He could be home sitting in front of a fire. Instead he gets a thrill, a dash of excitement watching thirty-six men fighting over a pigskin. He is unrecognized, unloved, but he keeps it all going. He's the spectator.

Stacks on the mill

Spring	T. S. Eliot said April was the cruellest month. In Australia it's September. Once again your team has failed to make the final five. Your conversations in the office washroom are starting to take on a stilted form. You can't keep on saying 'Just wait until next year.' You have done that for the past five. You wonder if it mightn't be a good idea to switch allegiance. Why not? Barassi has changed his allegiance more often than Zsa Zsa Gabor. You might as well go to the Grand Final. After all, you bought the darned tickets three weeks ago.
Stacks on the Mill	Omigod, my little boy is at the bottom of all that.
Statistics	The true enthusiast will not remember his wife's birthday. Upon questioning he will not recall the first name of his mother-in-law. But he knows for a fact that in the third round of the 1981 season Tommy Galah of Collingwood had fourteen kicks, six marks and seventeen hand passes, and went off five minutes into the final quarter with an injured thumb.
Straight Down the Field	The classic direct method—the shortest way home, or 'uptha guts'.
Streamers	A vital audience participation item. During finals matches it is the custom for cheer squads to plait a complete lattice of streamers in the club colours over the ends of the players' race, a task that can take three or four hours. The captain, leading his team onto the ground, bursts through the streamers to the screams of a hundred thousand spectators. Professor Ian Turner once described this as a piece of sexual symbolism, but then, almost everything is a symbol for sex.

Summer

A difficult season when the Australian goes into aestivation, as a snake hibernates in winter. Nothing happens. Occasionally he has to exert his intelligence to find something else to talk about. Admittedly, football news doesn't die. Coaches are always being fired during summer and ruckmen are always having babies. However, the sufferings of summer are well known. Usually under the nagging of his wife the football-lover has to put up a show of digging in the garden or painting the back shed.

Sunday

Once upon a time, in that distant past when there was no television, this was a sacred day. The citizens did things like going to church in the morning, mowing the lawn and pruning the hydrangeas and roses. Now, thanks to the marvels of modern science, football people can spend the entire day inside looking at the box. Such programmes as 'World of Sport', which pore over the previous day's agonies, are available in the morning. Then all afternoon can be spent, oh yet again, watching football.

Sydney

A place full of sin and incomprehensible evil. They acquired a team named South Melbourne, renamed them the Sydney Swans and (shudder) forced them to play on Sundays. The corruption has spread. Now for loose behaviour on a Melbourne Sunday it is possible to watch the Sydney Swans playing footy on TV.

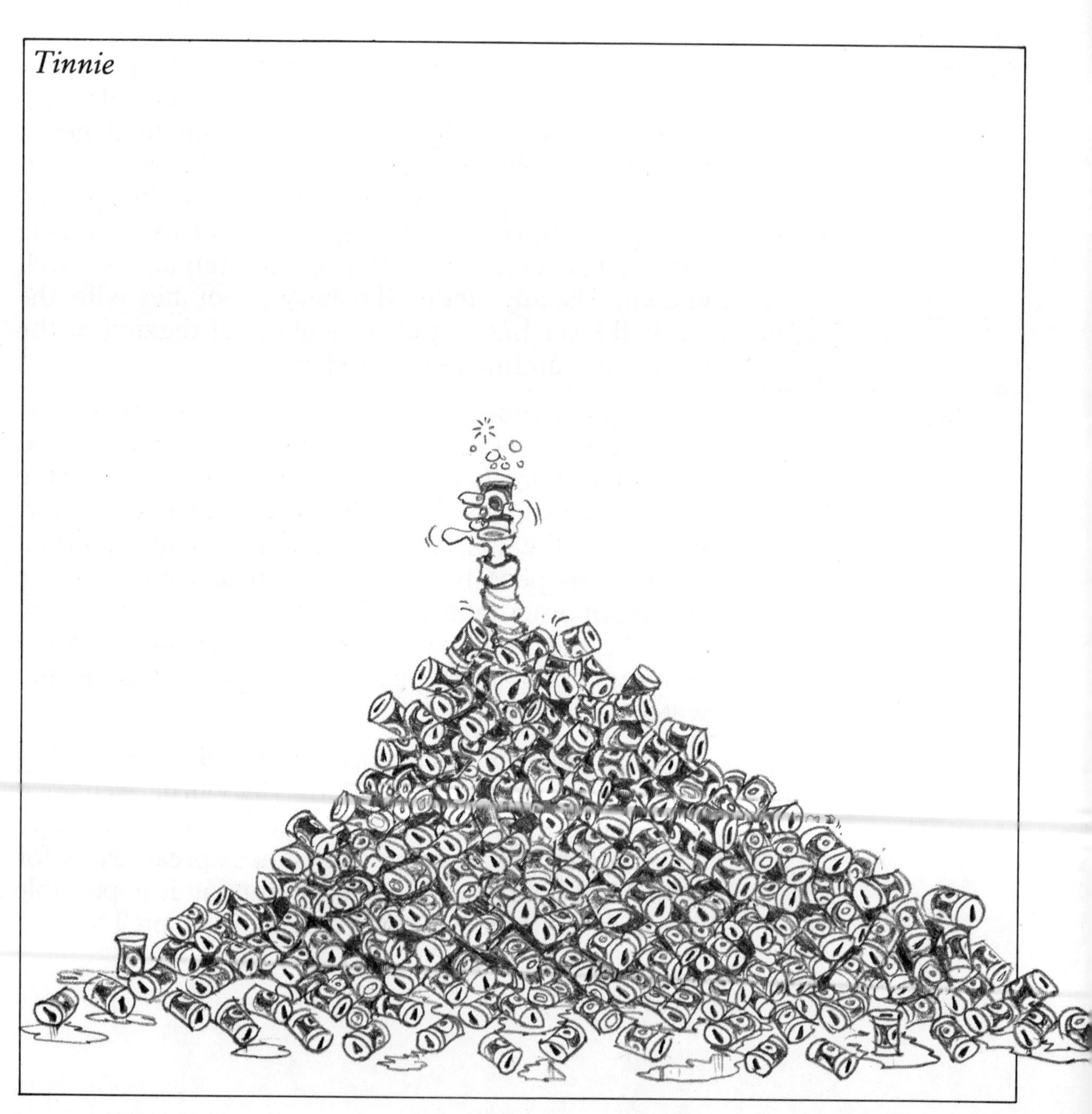
Tinnie

T

Tackle

In rugby this is done by assaulting spectacularly around the knees or simply biting the opponent's ear. In Australian Rules one tackles like a gentleman, with a bump applied shoulder to shoulder.

Tap Ruckman

The lofty ruckman who taps down the ball with peerless accuracy in the direction of his rover. If he is good enough at this you can forgive him for also being as slow as a brewery wagon.

Tasmania

An island off the southern coast of Australia, useful for the production of apples and as a breeding hatchery for Victorian footballers.

Team-building

Something you say you are indulging in after you have lost the first ten games straight.

Television

A useful method for financing football and a wonderful graveyard for old footballers. In most cities the football is played in the afternoon, then the matches are replayed on television in the evening. So you watch your beloved team in the afternoon, go home, sit in front of the box with your cans and see if what you thought you saw earlier actually happened. The suspicion is that eventually television will take over everything. There will be no need for live spectators and all that profanity, garbage and car parking. Football will be played on remote, secure grounds, and the entire excitement will be achieved electronically with recorded handclapping, boos and chants.

Transfer

Time On — A meaningful time of excruciating agony. You know the final siren could go in three minutes, four minutes. And yet, maybe we could make up those missing five goals. Miracles have happened before, haven't they? The followers could suddenly jell their teamwork into football magic, the forwards could become accurate for once, the rovers could recover their seeming lost youth . . . Please, God, don't let it sound yet.

Tinnie — An injection that used to make wet feet, cold winds and sore ear-drums almost bearable on Saturday afternoons.

Torture — After a bad loss on Saturday, coaches react with a fury usually reserved for wives who have just discovered their husband in bed with a chorus girl. Full-scale torture is set up for Sunday or Monday. Maybe they are forced to run to Ballarat and back in their bare feet, maybe they are forced to do two thousand push-ups, and in extreme cases they are even deprived of their footballs for three whole days.

Transfer — An exciting system of white slavery, where important muscle can be bought, sold or leased for prices ranging up to $300,000. Sometimes the player also gets money.

Tribunal — Usually sits on Monday nights to hand down instant justice for all the misdemeanours committed on the football fields during the week-end. Why Monday night? Well, nothing ever happens on a Monday and this is immensely useful for both newspapers and television. A ruckman leaving VFL House in tears can be guaranteed a five-column picture on page one.

Members of the League Tribunal have little learning but their decision has more impact and serious importance than anything handed down by the learned knights of the Australian High Court. Players are reported on the Saturday by umpires, boundary umpires, goal umpires and such. They give the evidence. The accused always pleads innocence, even though three million people have savoured the incident remorselessly played over and over again with slow motion replays on Saturday night and Sunday morning TV. The victim, even though he may appear with black eye and crutches, will always adhere to 'club rules'. That is, he is unaware of being struck. Indeed the accused is a good fellow who never had anything but kindly intentions towards him. After the club's star has been suspended for six matches, coach and even captain accuse the tribunal of savage anti-club bias against their innocent star. They threaten legal action, which of course never works.

Turncoat

A quisling, a creature who likes to be with the strength. By July or August the creature notes which team is likely to be on top by July or August. As they used to say of deviating Protestants: 'My dear, she has turned.'

Twin Flags

Once the radio men would say 'The umpire has raised the twin flags for a major,' but the voice men with a keener ear for a cliché now report that 'He's waving the twin calicos for a sausage roll.'

Umpires

U

Umpires — The men in white. They are so beloved by Australian Rules supporters that clubs provide them with races covered with iron grilles through which they run to get onto the ground. This is to protect them from the loving attention of their fans, who so admire their work they want to pat them over the head with bottles and cans. Umpires do have the advantage in that they always finish the game with one friend, the winning coach. Like highwaymen, bushrangers, bomb disposal experts, safe-robbers, parachute jumpers, tightrope walkers, shark photographers, movie stuntmen and sword swallowers, they don't last beyond their thirties. It is a wearing, hazardous profession.

Unlimited Potential — You haven't won a game all year.

Utility Player — They have tried him as full forward, they have tried him in the centre, the wing, full back and even in the ruck. Actually he isn't much use in any position.

V

VFL Players Association — This is the players' union. It fights for higher wages and better conditions. By 1990, players hope to win shorter working hours and longer breaks between quarters. By taking collective action, 100 minutes of football eventually will come down to twenty, with one-hour recreation breaks between quarters.

Victoria

Wife

Victoria In Victoria they are known as the 'Mighty Vics'. A Victorian team usually will consist of one native-born Victorian and seventeen South Australians, Western Australians, Tasmanians and Queenslanders. The players are lured by big money, so in Adelaide or Perth frequently the Mighty Vics are known as the Vile Vics or the Villainous Vics. In recent years there have been State-of-origin matches, in which players are dragged back from Melbourne to play for their home State, often a traumatic experience for all concerned.

W

Waverley An ingenious method devised by the Victorian Football League not only to snub the Melbourne Cricket Club but also to make life easier for the rest of us. It concentrates most of Melbourne's motor cars in one spot on Saturday afternoons in a splendid traffic jam.

Whinge When you are ten goals down at half time, when your premier ruckman hasn't had a knock-out all day, when your full forward has goose pimples from long, stranded inactivity, then the verb *to whinge* means the pitiful scream of complaint from the coach.

Wife An appendage. She picks up the bruised wreckage on Saturday nights. She listens to coaches' orders that sex is not acceptable on Friday nights. A footballer husband, inevitably, is too tired anyway. For six months she is a widow, the garden is never done, no messages are ever run, no intelligent conversation is ever uttered, she never goes anywhere. There is one compensation: should she ever produce a baby, should she ever get divorced, should she ever in a fit of frustration stick a knife into the gizzard of her husband, she will make page one. After all, she is the wife of a footballer.

Wing

There are two wing-men. If you despise one of them particularly you can always make sure the play goes down the other side.

Winter

A very peculiar time when people in football cities have to be handled with care. You can't expect them to arrange any appointments on Thursdays, Fridays, Saturdays, Sundays or Mondays. On Thursday there is that sacred time when the clubs choose their teams. On Friday there is the grave importance of taking in the previews. Saturday is lost, of course, with not only the game itself but the replay afterwards. Sunday is devoted to the post-mortems in the morning and footy TV in the afternoon. Monday, that's probably the most serious day of all. You have to stand by while your man is crucified at the Tribunal. My God, I forgot! I can't see you on Tuesday—there's the night football. There's just a chance I can fit you in on Wednesday, except I might have to watch the training.

Wooden Spoon

This is the team that finishes at the bottom of the ladder. It is not to be despised. There are certain passionate masochists who always seek out the team that is likely to run last. There are a hundred thousand turncoats who switch to the team that clearly is going to take the flag. However, there is prestige to be gained

Zoning
COLLINGWOOD, MATE –
AND STEP ON IT!
TAXI

in seeming to display a dogged Dunkirk type of loyalty in staying with a team that is doomed to failure.

X

X-Ray
A marvellous device invented by Madame Curie and others for looking at footballers' bones. You know almost immediately whether your boy is out for a month or whether you can throw him in for another bone-breaking experience next Saturday.

Y

Yahoos
You get a whole mob of them around Bay 21. It's amazing how they change their names with the seasons —bodgies, yahoos, yobbos, larries, houns, ockers— but their habits remain the same.

Z

Zealot
A crazed religious fanatic. In other words, a follower of Australian Rules football.

Zoning
Like the Hitler Youth, as soon as a male child is born he is destined to a certain flag and has to swear allegiance. Yes, the country is cut up into zones. It is a nasty system that always gives the other clubs the best players.